ENERGY WORK
—101—

ENERGY WORK
—101—

TODD CUNNINGHAM

BALBOA.
PRESS
A DIVISION OF HAY HOUSE

Balboa Press books may be ordered through booksellers or by contacting:

Balboa Press
A Division of Hay House
1663 Liberty Drive
Bloomington, IN 47403
www.balboapress.com
1-(877) 407-4847

ISBN: 978-1-4525-4199-0 (sc)
ISBN: 978-1-4525-4200-3 (hc)
ISBN: 978-1-4525-4198-3 (e)

Library of Congress Control Number: 2011919625

Because of the dynamic nature of the Internet, any web addresses or links contained in this book may have changed since publication and may no longer be valid. The views expressed in this work are solely those of the author and do not necessarily reflect the views of the publisher, and the publisher hereby disclaims any responsibility for them.

The author of this book does not dispense medical advice or prescribe the use of any technique as a form of treatment for physical, emotional, or medical problems without the advice of a physician, either directly or indirectly. The intent of the author is only to offer information of a general nature to help you in your quest for emotional and spiritual well-being. In the event you use any of the information in this book for yourself, which is your constitutional right, the author and the publisher assume no responsibility for your actions.

Printed in the United States of America

Balboa Press rev. date: 12/19/2011

CONTENTS

    Basic functions of the physical, mental, emotional, and
    ethereal human energy fields

    Aligning your cosmic energy (your higher self) with
    your physical presence
    Exercise 1: Grounding and Expanding Your Awareness.

    Becoming aware of your physical and emotional feelings
    and sensations
    Exercise 2-A: The Personal Sensation and Inventory
               Technique

For my grandmothers, Margaret and Julia, who continue to guide me, even in their passing.

"Faith healing is gaining your faith in yourself that you will heal."

—Reverend Roseann Joy Mason

FOREWORD

I have been a client studying and practicing energy healing work with Todd Cunningham since March of 2000. When I was two years old, my parents put me in a cellar where I was severely abused. I was thirty years old when I finally escaped from them.

By then, I weighed 640 pounds. I have become aware that I was using my weight to physically keep people from getting near me. My body size gave me a literal barrier that people could not get past. I had uncontrollable diabetes, high blood pressure, heart problems, post-traumatic stress syndrome, depression, fear of being around people, and high cholesterol. My doctor told me to start walking or I would have to go into the hospital. So I started doing little walks, out my door and back in.

Then I found Todd. I happened to see his office. My intuition overcame my fear, and I made an appointment for energy work. I began to learn grounding techniques, and I started to gain faith in myself. I lost three hundred pounds very quickly; most of the weight was emotional baggage that I released by allowing myself to feel my true self, my health improved.

Todd has taught me a lot, how to be myself, grounding, and how to love myself. This gave me the ability to believe in myself, and to just keep going.

I continue to work with Todd. It's eleven years later. I'm now 190 pounds, and I'm much healthier these days.

I have discovered that I have extrasensory abilities of my own, and they have improved greatly as I have practiced grounding.

Todd has generously shared his knowledge and energy healing methods with me. You will also find that these methods help guide you into yourself on your journey of becoming highly conscious and aware. Grounding is a partnership with yourself; you, your higher self, and our Earth. When things seem to be out of your control, the solutions are inside your own body, mind, and spirit. Just ground. You have everything you need within yourself.

Thank you, Todd,
—Rev. Roseann Joy Mason

PREFACE

I have written this book to help people learn to be consciously aware of and operate their personal energetic systems. I have not written this manual as proof or validation of the existence of human energetics. The science of our energy systems and their functions is in its preliminary stages. I have chosen to write from the basis of my personal functional experience, and I do not claim that someday all I present here will become actual scientific fact.

My point is, if you are reading *Energy Work 101* to obtain universal truths for a foundation onto which you can build your latest belief system, then you have chosen the wrong book. If you are searching for models of understanding and exercises that you can practice to deepen your awareness and relationship with the extrasensory information you experience, then you are likely to receive something from *Energy Work 101*. I am offering *a way,* rather than *the way,* to become more conscious, more aware, more efficient, and therefore healthy and happy.

I remind you that all scientific statements are theories, and some scientists seem to continually make the mistake of believing that theories are fact. For example, in the last 150 years or more, science has claimed that there was no life in the depths of the ocean because it was too dark, too cold, and there was too much water pressure. Well, in short, this is wrong. I concede that some of what I present in this manual will be considered inaccurate in the future. I present my energy workbook as a model from which you can learn to obtain your own information about our universe.

I theorize that we have a physical body made from the Earth and a cosmic awareness that is made of multidimensional energy fields. Yes, the Earth is made of multidimensional energy as well, but let's not confuse things right now. This cosmic light body is best described in English with words such as higher self, soul, and spirit. It is part of the all one universe sometimes described as zero point energy, God, Great Spirit, Brahman, Hado, and universal source energy. The energies that run your physical body have been described over time as ether, prana, qi, meridians, chakra system, and life force. I also suggest that your higher self does not need a physical body to exist. Although your physical body will function more efficiently if you make a conscious effort to become aware of your cosmic self.

Furthermore, here are a few ideas to speed up your conscious awakening. If you have an earthly body and your higher self exists independently of this body, then whether you remember it or not, you consciously chose to come here to Earth and incarnate into your present physical self. Therefore, commit to your experience by becoming fully conscious in your body here and now. I suggest to you that it is a cosmically coveted gift to be granted a physical Earth experience, including fear and pain, hot and cold, et cetera. Your primary purpose is to ground universal love and joy through yourself and into the Earth and this plane of reality.

With this in mind, you can stop searching for your life purpose and start searching for what you will be happy with, and you will find this internally not externally.

If my theories have any merit at all, then when you become grounded and aligned with your physical body and you pursue your true happiness, you will be anchoring this experience into the energetic field of the Earth. If this is true, you are anchoring your love and joy into the Earth, and you are actually increasing the potential for the rest of the human race to do the same. This may very well bring on a true shift in consciousness. I caution you to focus on your personal internal experience, rather than trying to save the world or fix the universe. By the way, our universe is whole and well now.

What I explain in these next pages is how I have learned to see and feel my higher self and the process I use to increase my conscious awareness. I have tried to leave the exercises open so that you may make them your own.

ACKNOWLEDGMENTS

First of all, I thank all of consciousness, including my guides, the angels, our and all universal consciousness, our earth's consciousness, and all individual conscious awareness past and present for showing me by persistently filtering through me that we are truly all one.

I thank my father, Thomas, for teaching me to examine myself and my involvement in any situation.

I thank my mother, Cynthia, for always supporting me in being me.

I thank all of my large extended family on both sides, for choosing to come here to Earth and allowing me to have our amazing family.

Thank you, Roseann Mason, for showing me that I am not the only one who has extrasensory experiences.

I thank all of my peers, clients, and instructors who have allowed me to learn my art through practice, especially Cathy, Roseann, Beth, Frank, Michael, and Steve.

Thanks also to Steven Breda, Brenda Giffen, and Carrie White, for their honest and supportive criticism of my manuscript.

INTRODUCTION

A Brief Overview of Your Human Energetics

Primarily, energy healing work is about consciously operating your own energetic system. Energetic healing is dependent on consciously maintaining your physical, mental, emotional, psychic and ethereal boundaries. Secondly, you cannot heal another individual. You can only be a model for them to follow in their own healing.

You are not meant to run or channel universal energy through others. They are meant to channel universal energy through themselves. As a facilitator, you can only be effective by consciously and powerfully operating your own system. Use yourself as an example to help other individuals more consciously experience themselves.

Ultimately you have your own unique energy system with a unique organization of common universal human energetic systems. Your energy system is a synchronization of three basic energy systems. These are your physical self (physical energy field), your mental-emotional self (thought, feeling, and belief energy fields) and your higher self (individual, ethereal energy fields).

Physical Energy Field

You have a physical energy field, and it is the energy field emitted by the chemical processes that maintain your physical body. In this way, each cell in your body acts as a battery. It is also the field produced by the activity of each atomic particle in your physical body.

Your physical energy field is also part of the Earth's physical energy field. You and the Earth share the material in your body simultaneously. The atoms that construct your physical body are constantly flowing between you and the Earth in a circle. For example, you breathe air molecules in and other air molecules out.

Mental and Emotional Energy Field

You also have energy fields that carry all of your mental and emotional processes. Thoughts and emotions are multidimensional electromagnetic energy fields. They are carried within your physical energy fields, as well as existing independently. In the end, only the most personal information is actually kept private. If you practice the exercises in this manual, you will soon discover that most thoughts and ideas are shared in the psychic universal energy fields. In other words, most thoughts are held in a collective consciousness or come directly from higher universal consciousness. This is a massive subject, one that can and does fill volumes of books.

Universal consciousness is the source of new information and the reason why a scientist in the United States and one in Russia can develop parallel theories and discover the same information independently. It is very important to understand, while developing your conscious boundaries that your thoughts do not necessarily independently arise but rather are actually linked to a mass consciousness, a universal consciousness, and an Earth consciousness. These are all multidimensional energy fields. Therefore, the two scientists who independently came up with the same ideas did not make up these ideas in a vacuum. These scientists were able to be conscious enough to receive ideas new to the human race from universal information about their subject of study. Your thoughts and ideas are coming from the universe and the collective consciousness and are not originating for the first time, but are influenced by your conscious awareness.

Beliefs and social customs are very powerful because of their ability to influence one's thoughts. You are a receiver of information from both universal consciousness and collective consciousness, and you have the ability to choose consciously, which is directly affected by your willingness to be aware.

Ethereal Energy Fields—Your Higher Self

Ethereal energy fields are those parts of you that exist without your physical body and independent of four-dimensional time and space. These energy fields are the eternal part of you, your higher self. To begin to consciously experience your higher self, you must first allow yourself to be aware that there is a part of you that has a physical body, as well as a part of you that is universal that doesn't require a physical body to exist.

Your higher self communicates with you through all of your energy fields. Therefore, your higher consciousness is communicating through your physical sensations, your emotions, and your awareness of extrasensory information. The first step in becoming more conscious and aware is to ground—becoming aligned with your higher self. Learning to ground yourself requires you to be aware of the physical and emotional sensations that you now have. Grounding requires you to experience what is true for you now.

Chakra System

Your chakra system links the information coming from your higher self, your mental emotional energy fields, your physical energy fields and the Earth's energetics. It synchronizes all of this conscious awareness into your personal physical being. Your chakra system is fascinating, and is the aura that many people first experience while opening to extrasensory perception. In *Energy Work 101* I focus on a dimensionally deeper, primal, and powerful system, your hara line. The reason being, when you align your hara—consciously connecting with your higher self and the Earth—your chakra system will naturally balance, and gain strength. Until you intentionally synchronize with your hara (your individualized universal identity), your attempts to manipulate your chakra system will only produce minimal effects.

Note: I have been purposefully brief in describing the functions and structure of our energy fields. The next nine parts and ten exercises are about how to become more conscious and aware of your physical self and how to align with your higher self. Though fascinating, the discussion of how your human energetic systems work is a different topic than learning how to operate yourself.

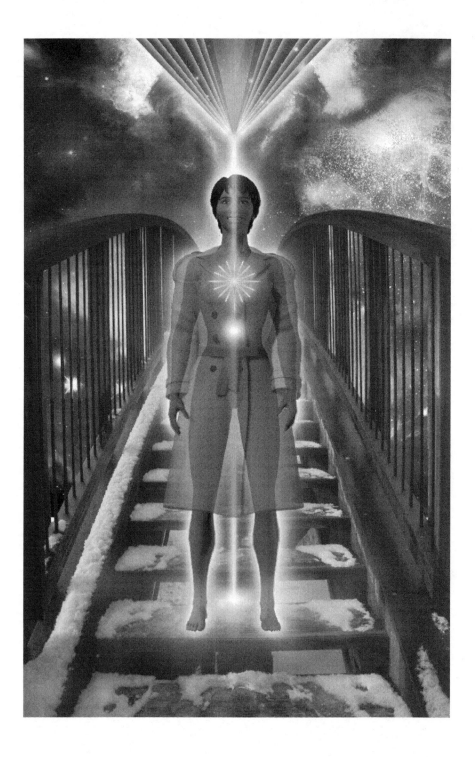

PART 1

Grounding and Personal Awareness

The first step in becoming more conscious is to get grounded. By *grounded* I mean bringing the energy fields of your higher self into alignment with your physical energy fields and body. Grounding is a multidimensional energetic connection between your universal identity and your personal physical identity here on Earth. It is the foundation of your existence in space and time, connecting you intentionally and energetically, between this present Earth reality and our multidimensional universe. It is the process that puts individual consciousness into motion and infuses it through matter.

What Is "Grounding"?

When you ground, you are anchoring your hara line into the Earth, *the ground*. Your hara line is a human energy system that is dimensionally deeper than your chakra system. It is a beam of multidimensional energy—including your individual, universal encoding—that is your frequency, your personal signature, distinguishing you from the whole of the universe. Your hara line has four very basic and powerful components.

1

Hara Line—ID Point

The first component of your hara line is your ID point. This is the point in space and time where your hara line—your specific frequency and identity—comes into existence from the whole of the universe. It is in the shape of a cone about two and a half feet over your head. If you have trouble seeing it, then remember that it is made out of multidimensional energy. If you practice the "Grounding Meditation" in Exercise 1, you will eventually have a perceptual experience with your hara line. All of the exercises in this book are designed to help you strengthen your connection with your higher self.

Hara Line—Ground

When operating efficiently, your hara line—your individual frequency—comes into this time and space through your ID point, passes through your physical self, and anchors into the core of the Earth, *the ground*. Your hara line is an energetic connection between the pure potential of our universe and the Earth. You are a physical manifestation of the combination of our "all-one" universe and your individual existence—which, of course, is made out of our all-one universe. Your physical body is made out of Mother Earth. You are not just made out of Earth. The Earth still consciously claims your body as part of her now. You are part pure universal potential, part individual universal identity (your higher self), and part Earth. As you look into this phenomenon when you call yourself "me" (I Am), you will find that you are an entire universal ecosystem, a coalition of cosmic consciousness that you experience as "me" (I Am).

Hara Line—Tan Tien

Your tan tien is located on your hara line in the area of your solar plexus. It is *not* your third chakra; it is dimensionally deeper. It is your physical, energetic and emotional center. The tan tien is the intersection of heaven and Earth; as above so below. Your tan tien is the intersection of all your energy fields and is located near your physical center of mass. This is your physical and energetic balance point. It is the point from which you broadcast everything you are intending to manifest in the physical Earth reality, both consciously and unconsciously.

Hara Line—Seat of Your Soul

The seat of your soul is the fourth and not least of the components of your hara line. The seat of your soul is found (dimensionally) beneath your heart chakra. The seat of your soul is the location—or more accurately the connection—your soul has with your here-and-now existence. Said another way, the seat of your soul is the part of your soul existing in this present time and reality.

No single one of these components is more important than the other. They have a circular relationship. If one is out of balance, then they all are. Also, the more powerfully grounded and aligned your hara line is, the more efficient the rest of your mental, emotional, and physical existence will be.

"Grounding" Is Consciously Running Your Hara

Your hara line is a beam of multidimensional energy, a multidimensional frequency pattern, and your signature. It is your individualization from the raw potential of our universe (zero point). Your hara line is your identity and your communication system with our all-one universe. Your hara line is that which grounds the universal you, your higher self, into material form. It is the location of your soul relative to your physical reality. The hara line is the energetic system where you radiate your intentions to the rest of material creation through your tan tien. When you ground, you are connecting your universal self to your earthly existence here and now.

> Note: Grounding happens continuously now. You have to intend to be grounded.

The more consciously you ground, the more your higher self will exist within your physical boundaries. Through grounding, you are consciously locating your universal self within your physical body in present time. You are aligning your universal energy bodies with your physical and emotional energy bodies. (These are your light bodies that correspond with your chakras.) You are claiming to the universe that you are here on Earth. You are consciously giving permission for your higher self to align with your physical existence. Consciously grounding will cause you to be more aware of your self and your surroundings. It will strengthen your perception of your environment. You are giving the universe permission and the ability to help you because you have consciously claimed your existence here, now.

Universal Acknowledgment of Individual Free Choice

Our conscious universe operates with respect for free will; you must grant the universe (God) conscious permission to help you (this is cocreation). Individual, universal sovereignty is maintained through the protection of free personal choice. Without this truth, individual consciousness would not be possible. Anything done to an individual without his or her conscious choice is an infringement on the individual's universal right of free choice. **All advanced consciousness must respect universal free choice in order to remain highly consciously aware.** Therefore, you must ask for help from higher consciousness to receive it. You must give your conscious permission for your higher self to fully inhabit your physical body. Grounding is the single most important choice and step in becoming highly conscious. The more grounded you are, the more efficiently you will function, mentally, emotionally, and physically. As you become more grounded, you will find, increasingly, that you always have choice. Even the act of not choosing is a choice. When you take responsibility for all of your choices, especially the difficult ones, you will be on your path to living more consciously.

Grounding and aligning your hara is a practice similar to a martial art such as tai chi or chi gong. It can be easily incorporated into physical movement such as yoga or walking. Practicing grounding and hara alignment is the practice of intentional conscious awareness. Grounding is the core of facilitating energy work because like energy follows like energy. The most powerful thing an individual can do to facilitate another is to ground in their presence. In this way, you become a mirror in which individuals may experience themselves. Practice grounding until you can be consciously present in your body at all times.

Exercise 1

Grounding and Expanding Your Awareness.

Being grounded is exactly that, a way of being. It is not something that you obtain once and then have. When you prepare yourself and your space, ensure that you are comfortable and you have privacy. Use aromatherapy or any other relaxation techniques to help you focus during the grounding meditation. If you enjoy music, use your favorite relaxation music with no distracting lyrics. If you are an outdoor person, go to your favorite place in nature to do this exercise.

All of the exercises in this book revolve around grounding. When you start, you may have questions. Most of these questions will likely be answered within the process of doing these ten exercises.

One of the most common questions is, "When do I ground?" The goal is to be grounded always. To start, practice grounding whenever you find yourself thinking about grounding. This will lead you into practicing grounding when you notice that you are not presently grounded. Eventually you will develop an internal alarm system that makes you aware that you have just disconnected from your ground. Grounding is a way of being and therefore an ongoing practice.

Another common question is, "How do I know when I am grounded?" The simple answer is, if you practice, you will begin to experience a shift in your sense of personal balance and well-being.

The actual sensations that signal when you are grounded vary widely and are as vast as people's abilities to receive extrasensory information. As you go through the exercises in this book, you will be cataloging your physical and emotional sensations. Through your experience, you will notice your state of being before and after you practice the grounding meditation.

In fact, one of the blocks in your way of being grounded and more consciously aware may be the belief that you need to know how you will feel when you become grounded before you actually practice grounding. This is a fear (a need-to-know program covering up your fear of the unknown / unconscious) that is stopping you from trying. It is as unnecessary as thinking that you will know what it feels like to ride a bicycle before you actually try. One learns how to ride a bicycle by trying and failing, and then along the way you gain experience, and associated with your experience are your memories of what it feels like to ride. In this way, you will learn about grounding by practicing and often failing at first. As the saying goes, get back up and try it again; it's the only way.

Good luck, and be gentle with yourself. Remember, less is more, and judging your failures will only slow you down.

The Grounding Meditation

Give yourself permission to imagine. Use your ability to visualize, your ability to conceptualize—it is your thoughts that are made of multidimensional light, which have the ability to connect you consciously to the core energy of the Earth.

Note: If you are wondering what to visualize? The ultimate answer is—your experience and therefore your perception of what you feel, and see while being grounded is unique and personal. That being said, you can try picturing a beam of light or roots coming from you and connecting into the core energetics of the Earth. Paradoxically, it seems, the way to find your unique experience with grounding is to go looking for it with a predetermined notion. So while you practice grounding allow the imagery, and sensations that are yours, to filter through your consciousness. Eventually you will have your unique sensory interpretation that lets you know you are connected, through your higher consciousness, with our Earth.

Ground yourself to the planet, your Earth. Feel through your feet. Feel through the ground. Feel through the water and the rock. Go past the areas that have been disturbed by humans. Feel the molten core of the Earth. Attach to it. (More accurately, allow yourself to feel that you are already part of the Earth. Your physical body is made out of Earth.)

Note: It is important at this point to become conscious that you are now giving yourself permission to attach to the Earth at the same time the Earth is receiving you and giving you permission to attach to her.

Your energy is extending down into the core of the Earth and grounding you; intentionally and energetically connecting you and synchronizing you, with the Earth. At the same time, the Earth's energy is radiating out from the core and passing through you.

Note: It is important to remember that the Earth's energy is running up through you because you are connecting to the Earth, rather than you trying to draw energy from the Earth. Another way of understanding this is that you are giving first then receiving.

Now, stay connected to your ground. Extend your energy out into the galaxy and through the core of the universe. Feel this. Allow yourself to imagine. This is your energy.

Note: As you extend out into the universe, to prevent your higher consciousness from going out of your body, it is important to stay connected to the Earth.

Now you are connected to the universe through your higher self, your body, and into the Earth.

Note: At this point, you are consciously, willingly synchronizing multiple conscious awareness into one experience you call *me,* including your higher self, your physical body (physical awareness), and the Earth's conscious awareness.

Feel everything around you. Feel the floor. Feel the room. Feel if there have been changes in the energy of the room since you started this meditation. Feel the next room over. Feel the street outside. Feel the difference up the street versus down the street. See, hear, taste, touch, and smell, all that you are connecting to. Does your body feel different? Are the colors that you see brighter? Can you hear the frequency of the objects around you? Are you surprised that your ceiling feels different than your floor? Allow yourself to receive extrasensory information without editing or judging your experience.

Note: If you are practicing this exercise outside then; see, hear, taste, touch, smell, and feel, all of the interactions you have with the Earth, the rocks, the plants and trees, the animals, the water, the air and etc.

Keep your eyes open. With your eyes closed, you may experience all this as imagination. Having your eyes open helps you tangibly experience your present conscious connections with the Earth.

Note: Becoming powerfully grounded and energetically aligned requires constant awareness and practice. For now, allow yourself as much comfort as possible while you practice grounding. In Exercise 8, you will practice grounding during challenging circumstances.

PART 2

Intentionally Experiencing the Language of Your Energy Fields

Sensations, both physical and emotional, are the doorway to knowing yourself and your universal language. Consciousness runs all of your bodily systems. Your feelings are your higher self, and your unconscious and subconscious mind's attempt to communicate with you. Physical and emotional sensations are your way of interpreting your environment using your energy field. Said differently, sensation is the language of your energetic system. Before you are able to consciously operate your energetics, you will first have to become conscious of what you feel. I call this becoming aware of what is true for you now. **This is a very important distinction in becoming more conscious. Instead of trying to predetermine how you would like things to be, you must be willing to consciously experience how things are for you *right now*.** This is a major shift in consciousness.

In other words, you are not going to become more conscious if you are not willing to experience what is true in this moment. In fact, conscious awareness can only happen now. It is necessary and worthwhile to learn your own system. Your energetic system is unique, and you have your own unique internal language.

Your systems operate through your heart and being, not through intellectual control. Modern societies have put way too much emphasis and responsibility on our ability to cognitively map a situation linearly from A to Z. The first step in learning to operate and balance your physical and energetic system does not exist within the arena of understanding intellectually how your system works. The first step in learning to become more conscious, more balanced, and function more efficiently is in learning to allow the parts of you that operate these systems to do what they already know how to do; in other words, learning to get out of your own way.

Learning to consciously operate yourself exists much more in allowing and giving permission than it does in understanding and being in control. Your systems consciously know how to operate themselves. Your first step is being willing to see the truth of what you feel now, physically and emotionally. You will only become highly conscious if you are willing to see your truth—*now.*

Exercise 2-A
The Personal Sensation and Inventory Technique

The purpose of this exercise is to become more aware of the physical sensations in your body. The usefulness of becoming aware of all of your physical sensations is that your physical energy field communicates with you through physical sensation. If you are going to become more aware of these communications, you will have to become aware of what you sense physically in current time.

1) Start by doing Exercise 1, the "Grounding Meditation".
2) Find a blank piece of paper. You are going to make a list or a map of all the sensations you can possibly become aware of in your body. Use the outlines of a human body below if you choose.

It is not important in what form you record this information. It is important that you choose to start cataloging what it is that you physically feel. Through repeating this exercise, you will begin to see patterns about how your physical energy field communicates with you.

In the form of a linear list or on a map of the outline of your body, starting at your head (or your toes), record an inventory of the sensations in your body.

You will find that one part hurts, another feels good, and somewhere else in your body, you may feel numb. For example, your upper spinal area in your neck can be tight, tired, and have uncomfortable burning sensations, while your ankle may be calm and relaxed.

As you do this repeatedly, you may reconnect with information. For example, "My joints begin to stiffen and I get a headache when I haven't had water for a while." Once you have connected with this information, you will more than likely choose to drink more water. This is a simple yet profound shift in consciousness. You did not make it by researching how important staying hydrated is for you. You've made new choices by becoming more aware of yourself.

Note: Your research on the fact that your physical self is mostly water will help you stay committed to your choice to continually hydrate. In fact, consciously learning that your body is mostly water and the physical and emotional changes that you process in order to become properly hydrated is a perfect exercise to partake while you are doing all of the exercises in this book. Water is a profound substance on our planet; it has unique properties that sustain all known life. There are life forms that do without air and visible light, but they all require water. Furthermore, there is preliminary science that shows the performance of water is changed by the frequency (vibration) that it is exposed to. In short, water is yet another conscious awareness that you are trying to synchronize in the whole of you.

Here is the short story: you are mostly water because it is roughly 70 percent of you. You need about one ounce of water for every two pounds of body weight per day. So if I weigh 185 pounds, I need close to three quarts of water per day; that's eight twelve-ounce glasses a day. Water responds to frequency, including the frequency of your higher self. Nothing else counts; no twelve-pack of any other liquid will replace the water in your body, because it takes more water to get the substance—even tea—through your body than there is water in the tea. That does not mean other liquids are bad; it just means they are not water.

Do your own research into the importance of water, and at the same time, do exercises 2-A and 2-B and record all of your physical and emotional processes while you are teaching yourself something as simple as being hydrated. These exercises will change you consciously. They will prepare you to receive your higher consciousness and change your relationship with our planet. Interestingly, the surface of our Earth is also roughly 70 percent water.

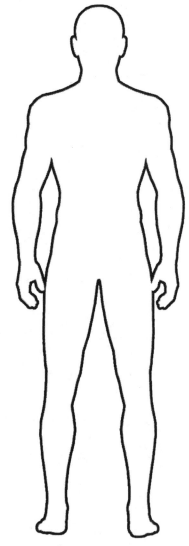

FRONT MALE

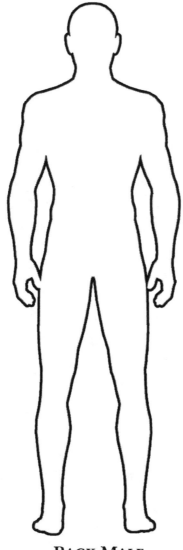

BACK MALE

Exercise 2-B

The Emotional Awareness and Inventory Technique

This exercise is very similar to Exercise 2-A. Remember, the goal of these exercises is to become more consciously aware of yourself. My first piece of advice is to avoid any desire you have to fix, change, or judge the information that you have received about yourself.

Emotions are energy fields that are contained and transported within your physical energy field. Your emotions are your reactions to your present environment, or they are your higher self attempting to communicate with you. Human emotional systems are so similar to each other that we can receive—pick up on—other people's emotions around us.

All of this can be very confusing at first. You will learn to distinguish between your reactions to your environment, communications from your higher self, and feelings you are picking up from other people by being aware of what you are personally experiencing.

Therefore, be willing to catalog your emotional feelings while resisting the temptation to fix, change, or judge what you feel. Over time, you will be more aware of your personal emotional patterns. You will begin to differentiate among your emotional reactions, your inner emotional landscape, and the emotional influences from others around you.

1) Start by doing Exercise 1: the "Grounding Meditation".

2) Get a blank piece of paper and some pens. Feel free to use some colored pens to make it more fun. Make a list or write randomly or use the outlines of a person to make a map of what you feel and where you feel it.

3) Yes, you will need to repeat this over and over again until you can do it constantly and instantaneously.

Note: It doesn't matter in what form you record this information. The power of this exercise exists within your willingness to experience yourself, without judgments.

Suggestions for Success:

Allow yourself to feel the emotions in any uncomfortable spot in your body that you felt in Exercise 2-A. Allow yourself to feel any fear you might have of what you might feel if you do this exercise. Allowing yourself to feel emotions that you have been ignoring and suppressing is the fastest way through the fear of what you might see about yourself. Document what you are learning about yourself.

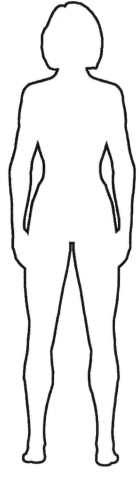

FRONT FEMALE

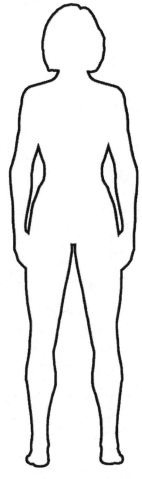

BACK FEMALE

PART 3

Practice Non-Judgment with Yourself

This step in becoming more conscious may be the most difficult. It requires observing yourself with non-judgment. This requires becoming conscious of how you feel and what you believe, to the point where you go beyond a limited view of your *self* and become aware of how you judge. It requires resisting the temptation to fix the things that you believe are wrong or bad within yourself. Becoming more self-conscious requires being conscious of your feelings and allowing yourself to be the way you are in the moment of experience. During this process, you will discover that the brave act of allowing yourself to experience your feelings is all that is required to jump start your built-in natural corrective mechanisms.

Your systems know how to heal themselves. You stop them when you block your experience of physical or emotional sensations. Once you are willing to be aware of how you feel, right now, you will naturally make new choices about any specific issue. Avoid focusing on what's wrong and how to fix it, because that will fog your perception. Instead, focus on what is, and allow yourself to experience this communication.

Now that you are practicing being grounded, you will feel and experience more. For example, you will feel more pain and pleasure. At this point, you have an opportunity to examine common beliefs, such as "pain is bad." In our global society, most people believe that pain is bad. The truth is, physical pain is necessary for your protection and survival. People who are born with little ability to perceive pain are in grave danger of injuring themselves repeatedly, often without even being aware of it. In its extreme, this condition can be fatal. Your pain is an opportunity to shift your belief and your consciousness. Pain is not bad; it is information that is trying to tell you something. If you begin understanding pain in this way, you will shift your relationship with pain. By embracing physical pain, you will change your relationship with your fear of pain. You will do this by simply being willing to feel your pain.

> Note: Although, I am using a basic example of pain in this discussion, the principles are true for chronic and severe pain. What I am suggesting is a conscious shift, from being afraid of your pain, to willingly embracing your pain. This will reconnect you with your higher self, and turn on your systems natural corrective mechanisms. Consciously choosing to feel your pain, discomfort, and the emotions that go with it, will help you heal. Hidden beneath your fear of pain, and behind the belief that pain is bad, is the truth about your pain and therefore, the causes of your pain. The most important information about any discomfort you have will be found within yourself, within the feelings that you dislike. If you have severe pain I suggest you start with something easy while you develop your confidence and experience.

Physical Pain

When you push pain away, you are actually disconnecting from your ground and misaligning your energy bodies. In order to suppress pain, you must disconnect the energy fields with which you feel pain. As soon as you are consciously willing to feel your physical pain, you will release all the energy you have spent on fearing and pushing the pain away. Now your energy systems can use this energy and the added energy of your conscious awareness to heal the cause of the pain. The pain, your pain, is a beacon of awareness, rather than something to run from.

Once you change your relationship with pain, as in the case of experiencing pain as information about your present reality, you will have a new physical and emotional response with your pain. You will begin to see the positive side of pain—that it is trying to tell you something.

Embracing pain and being willing to experience your pain and your fear of pain is different than becoming dependently attached to pain. Exercise 3 will help you change your relationship with pain, especially if you have fear of pain. It can also be used to change your understanding and your definition, your beliefs about pain. These changes will directly effect your physical and emotional experience of pain.

Exercise 3
Allowing Your Physical Pain

This exercise is extraordinarily valuable and the rewards for doing it far out weight the discomfort you will endure in the process. Also, the only way to learn it, is to do it.

1) Start by doing Exercise 1, the "Grounding Meditation".
2) Review the work that you have done in Exercise 2-A: "The Personal Sensation And Inventory Technique."
3) Allow yourself to go to the most painful part of your body or start with the least painful. Allow yourself to feel, see, and in any way, sense inside this part of your body.
4) The power here is in allowing the painful part of your body to have your attention and your awareness unconditionally. This means without judging the validity of the sensation or trying to change the present information.

Note: Be gentle with yourself when allowing yourself to be with this painful part of your body. Treat it as you would a young child who has been hurt. Avoid judging the sensations in this part of your body as good or bad, right or wrong.

This Exercise Is Valuable Because

a) You have just released the fear of what you may feel in a certain part of your body and allowed yourself to experience—now.

b) Your pain has been trying to get your attention, more than likely, for a long time. This area of your body has been trying to communicate with you, and you have just begun to listen.

c) By allowing yourself to feel this pain, you will release the pattern that is blocking your body's natural corrective mechanisms, allowing yourself to heal.

PART 4

Examining Your Emotional Relationship with Yourself

Emotional Pain

Emotional pain is very similar to physical pain—energetically. It takes a huge amount of psychic energy to wall off and store emotional pain. To avoid emotional pain, you have to disconnect your hara line. In essence, you force your higher self out of your body and encapsulate the emotional energy field, storing it in your physical energy fields and in your cells.

When you begin consciously grounding, you will begin to feel your emotions more intensely. They are not new, but rather, you are just starting to feel them. You will also feel more physical sensation. These too are not new. You are becoming more aware of your self. By being brave and allowing yourself to feel, you are allowing your energy fields to accelerate, align, and operate more efficiently.

Like pain, emotions are not good or bad. That is a judgment. Emotions are information that your energy field is trying to communicate with you. If you are getting angry, then it may be that you are becoming co-dependent with the situation that makes you angry. Your anger isn't bad, and it is telling you that you are feeling controlled by the situation. Your anger is telling you to consciously claim your boundaries. We will look at this more in Part 8, "Personal Boundaries."

Another example is sadness. Sadness is a normal reaction to a loss of someone or something that you were emotionally involved with. It is not bad. If you judge sadness as bad and repress it, you will be prolonging the effects of your loss, burying it in your unconscious mind and in your physical body. There it could eventually become a disease. Here your sadness becomes a fear and an energetic tax on your emotional system. Allowing yourself to feel your sadness will give you more information about the situation and allow your system to release this feeling.

Stagnant Energy Fields

Burying feelings—both physical and emotional—causes stuck, stagnant, and depleted energetic systems. Allowing your feelings enables your energy fields to begin flowing again, running more efficiently, and naturally balancing. An uncomfortable feeling is a limited energy field. If you allow your feelings, the energy will flow and eventually run out of your system. This stuck energy field will be replaced with your higher universal frequencies. **The highest frequency and strongest energy of our universe is unconditional love.**

Exercise 4

Allowing Your Emotions

By doing this exercise, you are practicing: (1) non-judgment of your feelings, (2) letting go of any attachment to your physical and emotional circumstances, and (3) unconditional love of yourself. Our systems naturally and universally know how to do the rest. This is how you generate, within yourself, a placebo like effect. This is true spontaneous healing, where the healing originates from within you.

1) This is a continuation of Exercise 2-B and Exercise 3. So, Yes! Review Exercise 2-B and Repeat Exercise 3.

2) Once you are into the most physically uncomfortable place you can be consciously aware of in your body, then allow yourself to feel the emotions that go along with the pain.

3) Do not judge your emotions that are attached to the painful area.

4) Treat yourself, as gently and unconditionally, as you would treat a young child. In this case, the child is you. (If you would treat a young child poorly, then you have a lot of work to do.)

5) Have faith. By this I mean faith in yourself that you can do this and that you will heal. Under your fear and your pain and your uncomfortable emotions are your natural universal mechanisms of self-correction and pure universal love.

Note: By allowing yourself to feel your physical and emotional pain, you are allowing the stuck and stagnant energetic patterns associated with your pain to begin to move and release from your system.

Note: Non-judgment and detachment from your emotions are two different relationships within yourself. Non-judgment is the act of allowing yourself to have whatever emotions that are present now. (*Acting on these emotions is a whole other matter, and having them does not give you permission to use them outside of yourself, as that would be a boundary issue.*) Detachment from your emotions is a form of denial that your emotions exist and a suppression of your emotions. It leads to disease and reflects the necessary energetic misalignment that is required to remain detached.

A REVIEW OF PARTS 1-4

Learning Your Unique Internal Universal Language

Don't Fix Yourself, Simply Allow You to Be Yourself and Allow Yourself to Feel.

Let's back up a little. One of the first steps for maintaining grounding is allowing yourself to feel. If you are practicing the "Grounding Meditation", then chances are, you are getting connected and grounded. As you become conscious of your feelings, you may disconnect. This is normal at first. The thing to do is to allow your feelings. That's right. Don't judge them and don't fix them, but just allow them to be. They are you, right? Desired or not, you created them within yourself. I call this getting to what is true for you now. *Now* is a very powerful place to be. The past is what's stuck in you now, and allowing it will give you power, from the present, to change your situation. The trap is judging what you feel as good or bad and then trying to fix it or make it go away. By simply allowing yourself to feel what is really going on in the moment, you will pop start your energy fields. You have just brought your unconscious awareness into consciousness again.

For example, if you allow yourself to be conscious that you are angry about a situation, you will make different choices than if you try to convince yourself that you are happy with your situation. These will be more truthful choices. Your energy fields know how to repair themselves, just as your heart knows how to beat. What causes your energy fields to be stuck and stagnant is not allowing yourself to feel. In order to not feel, you have to push these feelings into unconsciousness, and this requires a lot of energy. By allowing yourself to feel that which is true for yourself now, you will be able to make new choices based on your truth rather than manufactured belief patterns about how you should be. You are designed to repair yourself. Your system becomes stagnant when you are unwilling to be aware of yourself.

When you allow yourself to feel what's really going on inside of you, your energy fields will operate more and more efficiently and effectively. This means you will have more energy and ease of function. In turn, this will strengthen your physical health and increase your ability to deal with stress and challenges. You don't have to know how to fix your energetic system, any more than you have to know how your heart beats. All you are required to do is be willing to experience yourself.

PART 5

Differentiating Your External Sensations from Your Internal Environment

If you have been practicing your grounding, you will begin to experience an internal change. This is usually accompanied by a higher sense of personal well-being. Of course, you may first go through some anxiety and physical pain as you anchor your higher self into your physical body. More accurately, you will change your relationship with sensations. Your perception of feelings such as discomfort, pain, and anxiety will change from understanding these feelings as good and bad to an understanding that these sensations are information that your systems are trying to consciously communicate.

Note: Learn to collect sensory information about yourself, and instead of allowing yourself to react to your perceptions, teach yourself to use your feelings as data with which to make conscious choices.

In order to continue with Exercise 5 through Exercise 9, you need to develop an internal sensory relationship and visualization of when you are grounded. If you are having trouble sensing and visualizing that you are connected to the core energetics of the Earth, it is because you have not practiced enough.

Practice grounding until you can feel and visualize your personal connection with your higher self, your Earth, and your physical body. Remember that when you are experiencing grounding, judging success and failure will only slow you down and is most useful as evidence that you need more practice. Rather than mentally trying or forcing yourself to be grounded, simply *allow* yourself to be grounded.

Once you can tangibly experience whether you are in or out of your body, then continue with the next five exercises.

Exercise 5

Inventorying Your Sensations from
Your External Environment

1) Start by doing exercise 1, the "Grounding Meditation". By now you will be able to stay grounded and do Exercises 2 through 4 in current time. By being grounded and highly consciously aware of your internal sensations, you are remaining anchored in your body and present now.

2) Record an inventory of your external sensations, your perceptions that you do not experience as originating from inside of your physical self.

Note: Do this exercise as far away from other people as you can be, we will work with sensing another person in Exercise 9.

For example, notice that the grass feels different from the buildings, which are different from a tree, which is all different from the pavement. You are differentiating your internal sensations from your external experiences. You will next be able to notice how you react internally to your external environment. This is the beginning of experiencing where your boundary ends and your external environment begins. To further complicate matters, your multidimensional energy fields go through the lawn, for example, and the lawn's energy goes through you. Even so, there is room, multidimensionally, for both fields. By staying grounded, you will begin to sense what is uniquely yours and what is not.

You are now beginning to learn your personal universal language. Although most people's sensory abilities are similar, there is such a vast amount of extrasensory information that you will have your own relationship with your extrasensory abilities. The basic sixth senses are all extensions of seeing, feeling, hearing, smelling, and tasting.

> Note: I suggest that you practice this exercise over and over again before you begin to assign meaning to any extrasensory information you are receiving. As your experience grows, the transmissions from your energetic systems through your perceptions will reveal what they are attempting to consciously communicate. If you are patient their meaning will become obvious.

Inventory Your Sensations from Your External Environment

> Note: If you need help getting started, try to describe the difference you sense between one object and the next. Record what you experience differently when you hold a piece of wood versus holding a rock. You may experience this as an extension of your five senses, or you may notice a shift of your emotional state.

PART 6

Be Happy

Stop searching for what will make you happy. **Nothing will *make* you happy. Instead, become aware of what you will be happy with.** Of course, this requires first being willing to feel when you are happy and when you are not. A willingness to experience your feelings will allow you to be happy even when you are sad. You will be happy that you are feeling the sadness and understanding what caused it. When someone you are deeply connected to passes over, it is normal to feel sad, and allowing these feelings will allow you to more readily connect with the learning opportunities of their passing. Feeling your sadness and discomfort will allow you to feel the joy of their passing as well. Practicing feeling will allow you to rediscover the things, people, and places that you are happy with.

Here, you are practicing unconditional love. Unconditional love is a hyperconsciously aware state of being. Unconditional love starts within yourself, even when you are feeling hatred. Yes, I realize that I am describing a paradox. The alternative is to block your hatred and bury it in your unconscious so it can become a disease. Whenever people block their hatred, they push it into

47

their unconscious mind, where they do not realize that they are hating. Allowing yourself to love yourself and feel your hatred is different than acting on any feelings of hate. By allowing yourself to consciously feel your hate, you will have conscious free will to act, freedom of action. You will realize that your hatred is yours, and you will be less likely to direct it toward others. Keep in mind that to direct your hatred toward others, even if done unconsciously, requires you to channel it through yourself first.

Do That Which You Will Be Happy With

Stop listening to everyone's idea of what will make you happy. Stop running what you want to do through the filter of "what will they think?" Do those things that you are happy with. Not the things that you think will make you or "them" happy, such as, "How am I supposed to do it? What is the right way?" These are questions that may be limiting your experience of your true self.

Exercise 6

Inventorying Your Programming

Inventory all of your; I should _____, I shouldn't _____,
I need to _____, I'm supposed to _____, I have to
_____, They made me _____, I have no choice so I have
to _____, etc.

PART 7

Learning to Live Beyond Belief

Running Out Your Fear and Pain, Gaining Your Faith in Yourself that You Will Heal.

You may, with all of your newly conscious sensations, perceive that you are a mess, ground, and allow yourself to have all of your present feelings. Keep in mind that the sense of being out of control—because you are now feeling all of these things—is the same outdated program that is judging pain and fear as being bad. This is the *faith* part of faith healing. As my good friend the Reverend Roseann Mason says, "Faith healing is gaining your faith in yourself that you will heal." Gain your faith in yourself that you will consciously heal from the inside out. Have your faith in yourself that you can consciously handle your feelings. Discover that you are much more than your physical and emotional sensations. Physical pain, fear, anger, hatred, and disgust are all limited stagnant energy fields. They have been trapped in your body by your unwillingness to feel. If you allow yourself to experience your trapped sensations, they will run out of energy and will be replaced by your highest universal flowing energy streams of love and joy. You are not required to know how to fix yourself. You are simply required to be willing to be aware. Once you are aware of yourself in present time, you will naturally begin to make new choices and new relationships with your world. Be brave enough to feel what is your true experience now.

Believe in Yourself—Process Your Information in Current Time

Belief systems are dangerous in that, they are misleading, and they are filtering your perception. A belief system is an attempt to have a predetermined view of your reality, in the form of, "The world is this way." All predetermined realities are created within a fear of the unknown.

> Note: I am saying, we as humans are constantly making models in order to understand our reality, and then we make the mistake of believing our model is actually true. I am also suggesting, it will serve us best, to become fully aware of what our belief systems are doing for us, and how they hinder our present awareness.

Your belief systems are something you learned from your society or an external event, or they are something that you taught yourself. However it came to be, they are an attempt to have a predetermined way to operate in a given situation, a lens to view your world through. A belief system is a filter and a formula where you put in a situation and the answer is easily known. A belief system has a predetermined answer where, in a given situation, "I do (X) because I believe in (Z)."

Allow Yourself to Become Aware of Your Belief Systems

Saying, "It's all good." is as inaccurate as saying, "It's all bad." Simply, "It all is."

Instead of believing what your society has taught you, choose for yourself. Instead of having your beliefs—choose for you; choose for yourself with your current conscious awareness. This may be the greatest challenge and the most rewarding exercise in becoming conscious. It requires you to question all of your beliefs. It requires you to be highly self-conscious. It requires you to see, hear, taste, touch, smell, and feel all you possibly can about your present internal and external situation, both real and imagined. It requires that you choose continually in present time. Becoming highly conscious requires you to face your fears of what you do not know, and it requires you to become comfortable with the fact that you know very little.

If you want to be universally connected, then allow yourself to become conscious of the unknowns that you fear. This will bring you clear present-time information. When you are filtering present-time information through your belief systems, then you are filtering the information through fear. For example, if you have the belief that, "pain is bad", it is generated from your fear of pain. Therefore, you are filtering your sensation of pain through your fear of pain, which distorts your perception of pain, and connects these feelings to experiences that are otherwise unrelated. Believe in yourself. Believe that you can know what is true for you. Instead of having predetermined beliefs, choose with the information you are receiving now, and have your faith in yourself to know what is true for you. Choosing to do what is actually best for you will truly feel best. To do this, you need to be connected with your feelings and what you consciously perceive, on as many levels as possible. Instead of following your old programming, choose being present now.

Exercise 7
Examining Your Belief Systems

There is a more highly conscious way of being than having your belief systems tell you how to operate in any given situation. Your new operating system is simply to be as aware as you possibly can be, making choices, not from your programmed responses, but rather from your heightened state of awareness.

Through, becoming aware of, and examining your belief systems, you will gain experience about how you receive and process information. This will heighten your conscious awareness, as does becoming conscious of your physical and emotional feelings.

1) Do Exercise 1, the "Grounding Meditation".
2) As in Exercises 5 and 6, catalog your belief systems, your social programming, and anything that you have taught yourself to believe. You will find a lot of clues about your belief systems and social programming in Exercise 6, "Inventorying Your Programming."
3) It can be as simple as "boys don't cry" or "girls are always polite and courteous." These are social programs that become beliefs.
4) Examine all of your belief systems and social programs, and ask yourself if they are true now or if they serve you now.

Inventorying Your Beliefs

Inventory all of your beliefs and social programming that claim "the world is this or that way" or "I believe _____ , therefore _____.

PART 8

Personal Boundaries

Learning Your Boundaries and Maintaining Them

There are many types of personal boundaries. There are physical boundaries having to do with your environment and bodily contact. There are social interaction boundaries, emotional boundaries, and energetic boundaries. All of these boundaries exist simultaneously and overlap each other. As you practice grounding and personal awareness, you will become more aware of your boundaries and those of the individuals around you. You will become more aware of your physical surroundings and your body's relationship to these sensations. You will become more aware of how what you take into your body affects you, physically and emotionally. You will become more aware of how you feel, physically and emotionally, around various people. You will become more aware when someone is trying to control you physically, emotionally, and psychically. And you will become more aware that your attempts to control people and events around yourself are based in fear.

Each individual chooses all of his or her boundaries, consciously or unconsciously. It is each individual's universal right to have free choice over his or her boundaries. It is also each individual's universal responsibility to maintain his or her personal boundaries and personal space. There are repercussions for allowing infringements on your boundaries, whether you are conscious of this or not. There are repercussions for infringing on another individual's boundaries, whether you are conscious of it or not. All boundary infringements are codependent relationships, and these mental and emotional relationships have corresponding energetic attachments between the individuals involved. All parties are responsible for their actions and for their lack of conscious action. You always have choice; you are responsible for every choice, and whatever you choose, there will be consequences.

Exercise 8

Practice Maintaining Your Boundaries

In this exercise, you have come full circle, starting with Exercise 1: the "Grounding Meditation". When you are grounded, all of your energy bodies are aligned, and therefore, your physical, mental, and emotional boundaries are intact. You are also allowing other individuals the personal space to operate their own systems. In fact, you can only allow boundary infringements if you are disconnected from the ground.

The only difference between Exercise 1 and this one is in intensity. Now you are going to practice grounding in personally challenging situations. In Exercise 1, I encouraged you to find yourself a private place, a place where you felt comfortable to support you in learning how to ground. Now you are going to bring grounding to your everyday life, especially your life's challenges.

Practice Grounding While:

1) You become challenged by a physical threat.
2) You are challenged socially.
3) You are driving in your car.
4) You go to visit your family; practice staying in your body.
5) You perceive that you are challenged.
6) You experience the feelings that tell you when you are out of your body.

7) You become consciously aware of your energetic alignment.

It is very useful and appropriate to learn to ground on a nice, warm, sunny day, next to a pond with wildflowers and birds all around. It is critical and life-changing to learn to ground in the middle of an ice storm while you are driving and the person next to you is in a panic. In short, if you stay grounded under stress, you will get more real-time information and therefore you will be able to make conscious choices faster. When driving fast on the highway, a split second of composure and information could determine life or death. Generally, accidents are just poorly made, unconscious decisions. If you remain grounded in tense situations, you will receive more information more quickly, and you will be in a more balanced state of awareness to act on this information. Also, the people around you will sense your composure, at least unconsciously, and they may have an easier time of staying relaxed.

Do not confuse this with controlling the people and situations around you. If you stay grounded and calm, you will be showing the people around you an example of how to maintain their own boundaries. You are still allowing them to make their own choices. You may be altering your situation, but keep in mind that you are grounding by tracking what is happening with yourself. Focusing on grounding to alter your external environment will more than likely result in you losing your connection with yourself, and you becoming codependently attached with the situation you are trying to control.

The skills you develop in this exercise are the same skills that are necessary in order to be a good facilitator. By being able to ground under pressure, you are staying connected to your universal information system while you are challenged. You are showing the rest of the universe that you are committed to maintaining your personal boundaries, and you will begin to experience extrasensory information from people and places that are beyond your personal space. It is your commitment to honoring personal space and freedom of individual choice that will allow you to observe patterns outside of yourself. Your pledge to allow others free choice will ensure that you are not trying to make their choices for them.

PART 9

The Basics of Being Consciously Aware and Facilitating

The Skills You Develop While Increasing Your Conscious Awareness are the Same Skills Required to be an Effective Facilitator

First of All:
Begin by consciously aligning your higher self with your physical body. You do this by visualizing your hara line coming from the core of the universe and connecting through your physical body into the core of the Earth. By doing this, you are consciously locating yourself in present time, here on Earth. You are consciously giving your universal cosmic energy permission to inhabit and to incarnate within you. You are consciously committing to and honoring your personal boundaries.

Secondly:
Allow yourself to feel the physical sensations in your body. If you are choosing to be more self-aware, you are going to feel more. Not more good or bad, just more sensations.

67

Thirdly:

Allow yourself to become consciously aware of your emotions. More than likely, there is an unconscious feeling or belief that is blocking your system's ability to self-correct. Open these blocks by allowing yourself to feel your emotions. You will probably have multiple emotional responses to any specific issue.

Lastly but Not Least:

Monitor yourself to avoid the common traps. If you are judging your pain and emotions as good or bad, you are in a common trap. Examine your belief systems to find where you learned these judgments. Allow yourself to experience yourself without judgment. This will take practice.

Note: If you are trying to fix something so the fear and pain go away, then you are in a trap. Allow yourself to have your faith in yourself and your new choices. Have faith that your physical and emotional systems are designed to correct themselves. Your bodily systems know how to repair themselves. They were stuck and stagnant because of your unwillingness to feel. Get out of your own way and avoid the trap of trying to fix that which you have judged as being bad.

Being a Facilitator

Now that you are grounded, you are defining and claiming your boundaries, and you are allowing yourself to feel consciously in the moment; now you are prepared to facilitate another's healing.

Be the Example

The main principle of effective facilitation is "be the example" taken to the universal level. By highly consciously operating your personal energetic systems, you are presenting the individual you are facilitating with the opportunity to follow your lead. By anchoring your Hara Line into the Earth, you are showing the individuals around you how to do the same. By being aware of your emotional and physical sensations, you are encouraging others to do the same.

I do not suggest that you control your feelings, but rather for you to be conscious of what you are feeling in present time. In the end, you are in control of your feelings by allowing them. At this point, you will be proficient enough with all of the exercises in this book that you are comfortable and experienced with any sensations or emotions you may have while you are facilitating. If your feelings are overwhelming while you are witnessing another's process, I suggest you resign from being the facilitator at this time. If you have consciously committed to allowing yourself to feel while you are facilitating, you will have changed your relationship with your physical sensations and emotions. You will be proficient at processing your fear of sensation, and you will have a new understanding of how your personal experiences are communicating with you.

Yes, Facilitating Is Operating Yourself

The more conscious you can be of your universal connections and your personal feelings, the more effective you will be as a facilitator.

Remember, you cannot fix someone else without infringing on his or her boundaries. The only alternative is to help that person heal himself.

There are two basic ways of amplifying your effectiveness as a facilitator. First, process yourself; the universe is all one. If you are processing your reactions, the feelings that arise, while you are in another individual's presence, you may very well be altering those issues on a universal level. In other words, the issues that you become aware of about yourself, while in anyone's presence, are the little pieces of the universe that you have earned the right to change because they are part of you. In this way, you are changing a piece of a universal pattern that is parallel with the other person's process. There are traps here. If you focus on the idea that you are changing the whole universe, you may get lost. The universe is a very big place. If you are focusing on processing yourself because it will heal the other person, you have already gotten lost and have become codependent with the outcome of that person's healing. Focus on processing yourself, and allow the universe to decide what will happen for the one you are facilitating.

Energetic Mirroring

The second way of amplifying your ability to facilitate I call "Energetic Mirroring". The requirements for effective *mirroring* are grounding, self-awareness and personal boundary maintenance. You can mirror your client's physical and energetic patterns. The basics of energetic mirroring are first, maintain your personal energetic boundaries in neutral, so that you are not pushing energy—running your personal energy through your client—or pulling energy—attaching to and absorbing the personal energy of your client. Secondly, observe—follow—the patterns you perceive with your extrasensory information. Resist the temptation of trying to change these patterns. Especially, monitor your judgments of what you perceive. By maintaining your neutral boundary, and observing your client and his energetic system, you will be helping him become more aware of his present state of being. This new awareness will provide new information with which he and his subconscious systems can make new choices.

By mirroring another's energy patterns, you are offering that person an opportunity to become more conscious of himself. You are assisting him in becoming more aware of his personal patterns. You are not infringing on his personal boundaries, and you are not trying to make his choices for him. Being an "energetic mirror" for another individual or group requires a skilled level of conscious awareness. Experiencing the best results of "Energetic Mirroring" requires you to: (1) stay grounded and universally connected within yourself at all times; (2) maintain immaculate physical, emotional, social and energetic boundaries while you are facilitating; and (3) remain energetically and emotionally present while you are being their mirror. **It is precisely your commitment of being personally aware and present in the moment that causes you to be a mirror for another individual's process.** The basic universal principle here is that like energy follows like energy. Just as panic can be contagious in a crowd of people, so too can the process of being balanced, aligned, and consciously present have a ripple effect on others.

Common Facilitator Codependencies (Traps)

The most common mistake in facilitating another person's healing is wanting the person to get better. One usually falls into this trap because either the person's healing will validate your abilities or you believe that if the person's circumstance get better, then you will feel better.

At this point, **I am stating that nowhere in this book did I claim that it is *not* possible to channel universal energy through yourself and into another person. I am saying that channeling universal energy for another person is a codependent human energetic relationship and will create a list of issues for all involved.** One issue includes sharing each others energetic patterns. Another is the misconception that the facilitator is doing the healing for the receiver. This misconception that you, the facilitator, have changed someone's patterns for the long term is codependent. Also, the idea that the facilitator is the one doing the healing is equally codependent. This is akin to yet another codependent idea: that you can safely and effectively take pain away from someone else.

Even the act of picturing someone healed in your mind creates an energetic attachment between you, the other person, and your pictured reality. First of all, you are making the judgment that they are not already whole as they are now. This is your pictured reality and not theirs. The simple act of picturing someone healed in your mind is codependent. By doing this, you are becoming attached to this person and his future. You are playing God and deciding that you know someone's best future. This discounts the individual and the rest of the universe. When an individual is able to picture himself whole, then he is prepared to heal, and you have actually helped him in a universally balanced way.

When you are able to see the perfection of your clients as they are now then you will be on your way to becoming a powerful facilitator.

"Grounding" Is Different than Attaching to Another Person

Grounding and attaching energetically to the Earth and the core of the universe is different from attaching to another individual's personal reality. The difference is found in boundaries and free will. You are allowed to attach to the Earth because you are part of the Earth, and the Earth still claims your physical body as her own material. Yes, you share your physical body with the Earth, even now. In this same way, you are allowed to attach to the central core of the universe, because you are part of the universe and it still claims you. You are an individualized part of the universe that is conscious of yourself. The individual you call "me" is not meant to choose for another. That is crossing the boundary of individual sovereign free will and leaves you in a codependent relationship with any other being.

You do not accurately know, and are not meant to specifically know, what another individual's higher self or the universe intends for him. If your desire is for him to heal, then *that* is your issue. You might do this so you can avoid feeling angry or sad or scared that, in your perception, he is not well. Possibly his healing will validate for you, in your perception to the outside world, that you are a good facilitator. Perceiving that he is not well is a judgment all on its own.

There is nothing wrong with feeling emotions about another person's pain. In fact, if you do not, then you have probably already blocked your own pain. To facilitate powerfully, however, process yourself in real time. Feel your own pain, and allow the other individuals the same. Allow them and the universe to choose their own outcomes. You will not fix you by fixing them, but you may offer them an opportunity by being yourself.

Intentions for Healing

The intention to help individuals experience themselves, to allow them and the universe to decide what will happen, is the most efficient choice and is the real power of facilitation. Personally, when facilitating, I ask the universe to receive what is for my highest good, my highest joy and my highest evolution and for the highest good, the highest joy and highest evolution of all who are involved at this time to be available. This affirmation allows for free choice and allows for events and possibilities that I am not yet aware of. It ensures to all the consciousness involved that I am only here to facilitate and opens the door for me to see patterns that would other wise remain concealed from me.

Any Reasonable Healing Modality Can Be Used Along With, "Grounding" and "Energetic Mirroring"

Massage, craniosacral therapy, chakra balancing, acupuncture, acupressure, conscious language, shiatsu, neurolinguistic programming, healing touch, reiki, and body electronics are just a few examples that can be used to mirror another's patterns. For example, when using craniosacral therapy as a tool to follow the patterns in a person's body tissue, resist the temptation to manipulate the tissue in any direction that you think it "should be." Allow the intelligence within the person's body to do the changing. What happens is that with the energy in your hands, you follow the patterns in the person's tissues. The outside contact offers the body tissue an opportunity to be more aware of how it is twisted. The body tissue, in turn, begins exploring ranges of motion that it had forgotten and becomes more efficient. All you did was follow the patterns present. In the end, it is more effective to use a hands-on modality to follow a pattern, allowing the individual's internal intelligence to do the correcting than it is to try to manipulate another into a form that you see fit for him. The person's response to mirroring may initially take more time than pushing him into changing, but once his inner intelligence has engaged, his corrective process will continue long after the treatment has ended. The individual is doing the re-organization from within. Therefore, the results achieved by the individual's inner intelligence and higher consciousness are exactly tailored for him and his higher self.

Exercise 9
Practice Facilitating and Being a Mirror

Once you are proficient with all of the previous exercises, this will be easy. It will work in conjunction with any reasonable healing modality.

1) Receive permission from another individual to facilitate him or her.
2) Ask the universe to receive your highest joy, highest evolution, and universal love, and for the other individual's highest joy, highest evolution, and universal love to be available for him to receive now.
3) Be grounded now.
4) Maintain your physical, energetic, and psychic boundaries immaculately.
5) Observe and allow your mental, emotional, and physical reactions while you are in the presence of the other person.
6) Stay present with any sensations you become aware of within yourself.
7) Observe the changes that take place within the other individual's system.
8) Catalog the intuitive information you perceive about this individual and his patterns, for the purpose of learning how you receive information.
9) Do nothing else.

Note: The ways in which we, as humans, receive intuitively are vast. The basic forms of extrasensory information are all extensions of our five senses: clairvoyance (seeing), clairaudience (hearing), clairsentience (feeling), clairgustance (tasting), and clairalience (smelling). There is an obvious sixth sense, which is our ability to feel emotions. It is virtually indistinguishable from our ability to empathize with other peoples emotions—to be empathic. *I think that science has yet to distinguish emotional sensation as a physical sense because emotions elude or ability to quantify or measure.* Personally I am still learning the psychic information I receive. By simply observing another person and his energetic patterns, I have had great success in helping him become more conscious, change his self-destructive patterns, and heal.

CONCLUSION

Again, this book is about how to operate your human energetic system. It is not about fully understanding how your entire energetic system works. This intellectual understanding would literally fill an entire university library plus hundreds of subjects that most universities have yet to teach. For example, you do not have to be a cardiologist to understand how to support your heart in operating more efficiently. You do have to be willing to feel your own heart. You will first need to be brave enough to become conscious of what you think and feel now.

Once you start the process of becoming conscious of what is true for you now, you will naturally begin to make new choices about what you are going to do in each moment. This is a true shift in conscious awareness and an entirely new way of operating yourself.

> Caution: choices made in order to create an envisioned future that you think will make you happy are choices made out of your fears about your future.

Make choices from a place of being highly aware and present with your truth, and develop your faith in yourself. In this way, you will be making choices that are centered in your heart (your body and soul) and driven by your whole self. These are the choices you will truly be happy with.

ABOUT THE AUTHOR

Todd Cunningham facilitates energy healing work with individuals and groups privately and through phone and online remote sessions. He instructs workshops including "Grounding and Personal Awareness," "The Power of Facilitation," and "The Specifics of Energetic Mirroring." Todd has a radio program on *News for the Soul: Life-Changing Talk Radio* about personal grounding techniques. He has been studying and practicing energy healing since 1995.

Todd graduated from St. Lawrence University with a BS in physics. He has a diploma in massage therapy and related healing arts from Dr. Jay Scherer's Academy of Natural Healing. He is certified in CranioSacral Therapy I & II and Somatic Emotional Release by the Upledger Institute. Todd has studied body electronics, aromatherapy, and chakra balancing and has been fortunate to experience some traditional Native American ways of life.

He has developed his own systems including; Personal Grounding Techniques, River of Life Therapy, Conscious Language, and Energetic Mirroring.

Todd uses his abilities of sensing human energy fields and physical patterns as a mirror to help people become more conscious, learn to heal themselves, and function more efficiently. He describes himself as a guide who helps individuals become more aware of themselves and their higher consciousness. "Healing is a side effect of being willing to experience what is true now."

Todd is a whitewater rafting and kayaking enthusiast and enjoys all types of skiing. He is based in the Adirondack Mountains of Northern New York.

ENERGY WORK
101

By Todd Cunningham
WWW.PERSONALGROUNDING.COM
TODD@PERSONALGROUNDING.COM

ILLUSTRATIONS AND COVER BY JOSH POTTER
JOSHP@YOUCOULDCONSULTING.COM

Made in the USA
Lexington, KY
04 April 2015